SECRET ELY

Michael Rouse

AMBERLEY

For Reg Holmes (1902–83) and Pamela Blakeman MBE, for showing the way and keeping me occupied in the endless quest to find out more about our city of Ely.

First published 2017

Amberley Publishing
The Hill, Stroud, Gloucestershire, GL5 4EP
www.amberley-books.com

Copyright © Michael Rouse, 2017

The right of Michael Rouse to be identified as the Author of this work has been asserted in accordance with the Copyrights, Designs and Patents Act 1988.

ISBN 978 1 4456 7588 6 (print)
ISBN 978 1 4456 7589 3 (ebook)

British Library Cataloguing in Publication Data.
A catalogue record for this book is available from the British Library.

Origination by Amberley Publishing.
Printed in Great Britain.

Contents

4

Introduction

I was born in Ely and educated in the shadow of the cathedral. I was excited when I opened any gazetteer or book and found a mention of Ely, but it was usually a reference to the cathedral which, in my childhood, threw a large grey shadow over the town. I did not have any understanding of the history of the town and like most small boys I found Ely a small, dull place, only coming alive on a Thursday market day. There was no activity on the river, it often flooded at Annesdale, and there was no footpath along the river from that quay to Waterside. But there was a choice of three cinemas and I frequently visited the Majestic, escaping to the Wild West with the Durango Kid or Hopalong Cassidy, or rode the high seas with Errol Flynn.

My good fortune came when I was eventually to be involved with the setting up of the Ely Society in 1969 and by then I had begun to realise that Ely was more than just the magnificent cathedral. The motivation behind forming the Ely Society was trying to save the ancient Waterside from wholesale slum clearance.

It was at the Ely Society that I met Reg Holmes. He was around forty years older than me and really inspired in me a love for Ely's history. For years he had been labouring on research in all aspects of the city's history, which he painstakingly typed up and had bound into volumes. One of the great achievements of the Ely Society was to bring much of this research into print.

We published two books of old photographs together entitled *Ely Cathedral City and Market Town* – Volume 1 in 1972 and Volume 2 in 1975. Such books were uncommon then and created a great deal of interest locally. Reg died in 1983 and Pamela Blakeman took up much of his research and carried on publishing local history, now through Ely History Publications. Thanks to all their work over the years I'm not sure that there are many secrets left to tell about Ely!

Having said that, of course, there are still a few, and *Secret Ely* shares some of the quirkier aspects of Ely's history not always covered in other books. For example, this book puts to rest some misconceptions about Oliver Cromwell, reveals where Highflyer is buried, and explains how to pronounce the area by the river known as the Cresswells, and it is my pleasure to share these with you.

1. The Island of Eels

According to the Venerable Bede, who lived from around 672 to 735, the origin of the name Ely was in the vast quantities of eels caught in the waters surrounding the small fenland island on which St Etheldreda founded her abbey in 673.

They were caught in their thousands and not only provided a source of food for the fen dwellers but they could also be used as currency, for paying rent and purchasing goods. It is said that the stone to build Ely Cathedral, most of it coming from the quarries at Barnack near Peterborough, was paid for in eels.

Ely has an eel trail with small brass eels set into the footpaths to mark the route and an eel sculpture in the Jubilee Gardens by Peter Baker, installed in 2005 and commissioned by the Rotary Club of Ely to mark the centenary of Rotary International. Eel glaives, the barbed pronged spears used to catch the eels, feature on the City of Ely badge and are depicted in another sculpture outside the Maltings.

The last of the Ely eel catchers, Sid Merry (1931–2012), was the third generation of his family trapping eels. He kept his boat and his nets on Babylon and in his lifetime saw the dramatic decline of eel stocks: today there is no commercial fishing for eels in the fens.

Peter Baker's eel sculpture in Jubilee Gardens.

2. Eel Day

To celebrate the importance of the eel in the city's history there is an annual festival – the Ely Eel Festival – established in 2004. There is a carnival procession and day of games and festivities which include the World Eel Throwing Competition; although it must be stressed that no live eels are used.

Eel Day Parade on Fore Hill, 2017.

Throwing the 'golden eel' during Ely Eel Festival, Market Place, 2017.

3. St Audrey's Well

On Barton Fields, on the edge of the golf course, near an area known as 'Hilly Pieces', once heavily excavated for gravel for constructing the turnpike roads, is a spring and a small pond that historically was known as St Audrey's Well (Audrey being the popular name for Etheldreda).

Etheldreda was one of the daughters of Anna, the Christian King of the Angles, whose realm covered most of Norfolk and Suffolk from his home at Exning. Although Etheldreda wanted to live a religious life she married Tonbert, a prince of the Girvii, the Saxon tribe that lived in the fens. This was part of a political alliance to give Anna some protection on his western borders from Penda, the heathen king of the Mercians. Part of Etheldreda's marriage settlement was the gift of the island of Ely.

After Tonbert died Etheldreda lived on her island but then was given in marriage again, this time to Egfrith, heir to the kingdom of Bernicia in Northumberland. Eventually Etheldreda left her husband and fled back south to her fenland island. In Saxon times there was a small settlement of Cratendune on the island. Its exact location has never been clearly established but it was somewhere to the west of where St Etheldreda founded her abbey. The building of the abbey in 673 seems to have led to Cratendune being abandoned.

St Audrey's Well.

Interior of St Etheldreda's Church.

DID YOU KNOW?

St Etheldreda's Roman Catholic Church in Ely has the mummified hand of St Etheldreda, which was brought to the church in 1953 by Father Guy Pritchard to mark the fiftieth anniversary of the dedication of the building.

4. Turbotsey

Etheldreda sited her abbey on one of the highest points on the eastern side of her island. The land to the east sloped rapidly away down to marshy flooded fenland through which larger rivers wandered because of the flatness of the basin, which stretches up to the Wash. There was a stream coming to the foot of the hill from Cawdle Fen near Angel Drove, but the main river was close to the foot of Stuntney's hill, some half a mile away.

The Saxon port for Ely was at Turbotsey, which was a mile away to the north-east and reached by Springhead Lane. The bed of the old river, possibly Rolls Lode, that once led to Turbotsey from Quanea, can be clearly seen against the dark soil.

Course of the old river from Quanea to Turbotsey.

It was to Turbotsey that Abbot Brithnoth brought the body of St Etheldreda's sister, St Withburga, when his party of monks stole her corpse from Dereham in July 974. These shrines brought pilgrims, and pilgrims were good for the local economy, so Brithnoth wanted St Withburga to join the shrine of the foundress.

Turbotsey became less important as the port for Ely when a new channel was cut at the foot of Ely's hill around 1100 to enable stone for the building of the cathedral to be landed much closer. There are records of a chapel surviving there until the sixteenth century and there were buildings which were lost when, in 1925, the Ely Beet Sugar Factory was built on the area of the old port.

5. Lovers Lane

One of the most popular walks for Ely people is a very ancient one indeed. Springhead Lane was once known as Blithinghale Lane and is one of the oldest tracks in Ely as it connected the Saxon port of Turbotsey with the medieval centre of the town. The first section of the lane from Prickwillow Road is a made-up road with houses on either side but the section on the other side of Lisle Lane is an attractive country walk linking to other walks.

Lovers Lane.

The old part of Springhead Lane is known locally as 'Lovers Lane', although on some old maps it appears as Lower Lane. Lovers Lane may be a corruption of this. It leads to Kiln Lane, which, as the name implies, was once the track to a brickmakers' kiln near the Roswell Pits, where there was a ready supply of clay. Nothing remains of those works today.

The land around the upper part of Springhead Lane was extensively dug out for shingle and ballast when Samuel Morton Peto brought the railway through Ely in the 1840s. As with Barton Fields, there are springs in the area and water gathers alongside the lane.

6. Roswell Pits

In the seventeenth century this area was known as Roswell Hill or Roslyn Hills, among other variations. It was a popular area for fishing and catching wildlife. After the main drainage of the fens in the mid-seventeenth century, under the direction of Sir Cornelius Vermuyden, the fenland soil which was a form of compost called peat, while being very rich for growing crops, also shrivelled and sank as it dried out. The consequence of this was that the rivers began to overflow so they had to be embanked. The best material for this was clay and the Roswell Pits area was one of the main sources of Kimmeridge Clay, known locally as gault.

Sailing on Roswell Pits.

The gault was extracted by gangs of gaulters and transported by barges. In 1947, following the floods of that year, a new pit was dug alongside Springhead Lane. The pits have not been dug for gault for many years and are now an important leisure and wildlife area. In April 2009 around 210 acres of the pits and the surrounding area became a Site of Special Scientific Interest, with some of it managed by the Wildlife Trust and the rest by Ely Wildspace, although the main pit and much of the land around it is privately owned.

Angling remains a popular sport in the pits and in 1946 Ely Sailing Club began in the main pit and continues to flourish as a member of the Royal Yachting Association.

The Commons that run along the top of the pits are privately owned: one part by Jalsea Marine Services Ltd and Milking Hill Common by Thomas Parsons Charity, but managed by the District Council. In 2013 the Commons were registered as a village green and are greatly enjoyed by walkers.

DID YOU KNOW?

The area of land north of the sailing pit was originally the Blue Lagoon, which was filled in during the 1960s after a tragic drowning in the pit.

7. Cuckoo Bridge

Cuckoo Bridge bridges the channel from the River Ouse into the Roswell Pits. It is on the old track which includes Springhead Lane that linked Ely to the port area of Turbotsey. There was an area called Broad Pieces where there were a few cottages and a pub (the Pike and Eel), but in the mid-1920s the whole area was occupied by the Beet Factory.

The gault from Roswell Pits was carried out on barges under Cuckoo Bridge to the main river. Until 1939 there was a stone bridge but during that year the bridge was struck by a barge and had to be dismantled. Two wooden bridges followed, until in 2000 a more permanent bridge was put in place by the County Council.

The bridge remains an important link for leisure walkers. It is possible to hear the cuckoo's distinctive call at the bridge, but no one is sure of the origins of the name: it could be a corruption of cock-up bridge, which was a bridge that could pull up the central section to allow barges to pass underneath, but I like the association with that increasingly rare bird.

Cuckoo Bridge.

8. The Cresswells

The River Great Ouse carried goods to and from the city. Before the railway came to Ely in the mid-1840s the river system was the vital transport corridor. For many the river also provided great angling waters. Either side of the twentieth century fishermen from Sheffield would come to Ely during Wakes Week and stay in local boarding houses for a week's fishing. For the people of Ely it was a welcome boost to their income and ensured the local pubs gained some extra business.

While fishing today is very much about the sport and returning any catches to the water, in days gone by fish and eels were taken in great quantities and were a welcome supplement to the fenman's meagre diet.

The area north of Commuckhill Bridge, known as the Cresswells, is a popular fishing stretch and still part of the Coopers Arms Fishing Club, although that Waterside pub closed in 1955 and was demolished in 1972.

Commuckhill is a contraction of Common Muckhill, which was the area near the bridge.

The Cresswells was an area where local people went to gather watercress, but since they called watercress 'water creases', the correct pronunciation is cree-sells. The Cresswells now forms part of an attractive riverside walk that links up with Springhead Lane to make a circular walk.

The Cresswells.

Commuckhill railway bridge.

9. Country Park

Ely's country park, managed by East Cambridgeshire District Council, is a Blue Flag award-winning open space providing walks, a children's play area and picnic space. It runs alongside part of Springhead Lane so there are opportunities for much longer walks, returning along the Cresswells.

Most people are unaware that this was once the city's refuse dump – the Common Muckhill – and nearby, in the area now known as Willow Walk, was some of the most overcrowded and poorest housing in the city. There is some evidence of a lost ditch or stream that ran down into the river along the line of Willow Walk and as this carried filth and sewage it contributed greatly to the insanitary state of the dwellings.

It is likely that this was an area excavated for clay, possibly for constructing the embankment for the railway lines which came through the area in the mid-1840s. Over many years the old pit was filled in with the city's rubbish until it became full in the 1960s. Positive action was taken in the 1970s when the Urban District Council and then its successor, East Cambridgeshire District Council, began converting the old tip into a new

Ely Country Park.

recreation area. For some years the Ely Society managed it as a Pocket Park, but around 2010 footpaths were laid down and play equipment installed as the District Council began the area's transformation into a children's play park and general recreation area. Since then more equipment has been added and the council continues to develop the park, which will be linked by footpaths and walks and eventually stretch around the western side of the city.

10. Paradise

Paradise is a much older sports ground near the centre of the city. Ely Cricket Club was given the use of Paradise Close in around 1855 and still plays there today. Between 1880 and 1892 Paradise was the venue for an annual sports day organised by the Ely Working Men's Club and Institute, which developed into one of the largest and most popular August Bank Holiday sports events for many miles around. Run by the City of Ely Sports Association, there was a full programme with athletics and cycling and often fireworks and a ball at the Corn Exchange to conclude the day's events. In 1903 some 8,500 spectators were recorded, in 1928 some 9,000, and in 1947, happy the war was finally over, around 10,000 people attended. Numbers, however, began to fall off dramatically in the early 1960s and in 1964 the last sports day was held.

City of Ely Cricket Club has been playing cricket at the Paradise ground since at least 1856.

In 1929 the original Paradise was enlarged when the adjoining Priest Bower Close was incorporated into the recreation ground. Paradise was the home of Ely City Tennis Club, Ely City Football Club and Ely Rugby Club.

In the 1960s the Church Commissioners, who owned the Paradise, were looking at the site for residential development but it was saved as an open space for sport and recreation when it was purchased by the City of Ely Urban District Council in 1964. Needing floodlights and better facilities, Ely Football Club moved to a new ground on Downham Road in 1986, joining the rugby, tennis and hockey clubs, but the Paradise, with the Paradise Sports Centre built along its edge, is still used for cricket and football, and, importantly, remains a vital green lung in the city.

11. The Park

Once part of the monastery, the Park must be one of the finest urban open spaces in the country, affording a classic view of the southern side of the cathedral. The Park is really three areas: the Dean's Meadow is closest to the cathedral and is used for grazing (it is not accessible to the public); the Park has been managed by the District Council since 1959 and is open for general use and civic and private parties and concerts; and Cherry Hill.

The Dean's Meadow.

Cherry Hill from the Park.

DID YOU KNOW?

The Park was once a monastic vineyard?

In the *Topography of Medieval Ely*, edited by Anne Holton-Krayenbuhl, the course of an ancient stream or open drain is shown as running straight through the Park and into the river.

Cherry Hill is the motte of the Norman motte and bailey castle that was erected after William the Conqueror finally drove Hereward and his Saxon supporters from the island of Ely in 1071. The earthworks of the bailey can clearly be seen in the Park. It was the first of Ely's two castles; the other, built by Bishop Nigel near the river in the twelfth century, was dismantled, leaving no trace. In medieval times Cherry Hill had a windmill on top of it, milling grain from the nearby monastic barn, which is now King's Ely's dining hall. In 1779 Canon James Bentham, who lived at Hill House at the top of Back Hill, remodelled the mound and placed a summerhouse on top, approached by a winding path. A monument in pseudo-Classical style and the words 'That this might benefit another age' was erected to commemorate his work. The mound was renamed Cherry Hill, as Cherry Sunday was a popular celebration in honour of the annual cherry harvest.

One hundred years later Dean Merivale planted an oak tree on Cherry Hill and added to the inscription that he was doing it in 'like manner regard for posterity'. Unfortunately, posterity brought vandalism of the column and despite restoration by John Ambrose on behalf of the Ely Society in 1985, there was further damage and it had to be removed into storage. Cherry Hill is currently fenced off from public access.

DID YOU KNOW?

The dips and hollows in the Dean's Meadow mark the old medieval fish ponds?

12. 'The Ship of the Fens'

Building the motte and bailey castle at Ely was one way that William the Conqueror had of maintaining his hold over his new kingdom; the other was a much more enduring legacy and symbol of authority – the cathedral. Etheldreda's original abbey, built in 673, was destroyed in the Viking raids on the fens in 870. The abbey was re-founded by King Edgar in 970, but William's plans were on a far greater scale. He sent Abbot Simeon, then in his 80s, to Ely in 1081 to begin work on a great Norman cathedral that would take over 200 years to complete.

Perhaps the most astonishing fact with the cathedral is that there is no local building stone. The island of Ely is an outcrop of upper green sand and what sandstone that can be obtained locally is suitable for infill or walls but not a massive structure like the cathedral. Barnack limestone was the main building stone and this had to be transported from the quarries near Peterborough. This is where the eels came in to help to pay for it and being surrounded by water and rivers helped with the transport, except that the port of Turbotsey was about a mile from the site of the building.

The solution was dramatic – to move the main river that flowed close to Stuntney's hill to the foot of Ely's hill. Surprisingly there is no date recorded for this work, which could suggest that it was not such a dramatic move after all. There was already a stream running into Annesdale from Cawdle Fen, so perhaps it was more a question of digging out the existing ditch that collected the water from Ely's various springs, open sewers and drains and turning it into a wide channel, then diverting the main river water through it. Whatever the answer is, that is how the River Ouse bends in to be close to the foot of Ely's hill and since the building stone was needed towards the end of the eleventh century, the new cut could have been made around 1100.

As the cathedral could be seen across the flooded marshy fens, it must have indeed looked like a great ship and recent warnings about climate change and rising sea levels have suggested that at some time in the future it may look so again.

River Ouse at Annesdale.

Ely Cathedral from Queen Adelaide Way.

DID YOU KNOW?

At the start of the Second World War it was debated whether to try and camouflage Ely Cathedral. It was decided not to and the building became a helpful landmark to airmen on both sides.

13. Jubilee Gardens

The riverside Jubilee Gardens were created by the District Council and opened by the Duke of Edinburgh in 2002.

The site had been home to various businesses including a fellmongers and more recently a wood yard, first as Alfred Wood & Co. and then as Jewson's. Historically the businesses ran down to the river until the Urban District Council acquired the land to construct the Riverside Walk, which by 1968 connected Quayside and Annesdale and created Ely's most

Jubilee Gardens bandstand, 2017.

Stone commemorating the opening of Jubilee Gardens in 2002.

popular walk. When Jewson's relocated, the site was cleared and in 2001 the television programme *Time Team* broadcast their investigations, revealing that it was a medieval dock and the place where the stone for the building of the cathedral was unloaded before being dragged up the hill through the Park area to the cathedral site.

The gardens link the Riverside Walk to the Park and Ely Cathedral. They also provide various areas for relaxation. There is a sensory garden and a children's play area. There is a bandstand and in the summer the City Council sponsors weekly concerts by local bands. The gardens are also busy on Ely Eel Day and the Rotary Clubs' Aquafest, held on the first Sunday in July when there are traditional raft races and other entertainment.

Cared for by The Friends of Jubilee Gardens and maintained by the District Council, the gardens are a Blue Flag award-winning public open space.

14. Babylon

A survey of Ely ordered by Bishop John of Fountains in 1222 refers to land 'beyond the water'. This is a reference to what has been called since the seventeenth century Babylon, no doubt a fenland nod to the ancient biblical city.

Babylon.

Lincoln Bridge over the River Great Ouse.

It could be surmised that there were people living and working on that area right on the edge of Ely's island who were cut off from the town by the diversion of the main river in around 1100. They continued to live there and were further isolated when the railway lines cut across their properties in 1845. There were twenty households listed on Babylon in 1851 but in the first half of the twentieth century the cottages gradually fell into disrepair.

Unless Babylon was approached by boat the only way across was by a chain ferry, which was stationed near the Annesdale boathouse and operated by the Appleyard family. The Appleyards built their boathouse at Annesdale in 1877, constructing boats in the small yard beside it. After the Second World War Harry Lincoln acquired the company and it became Appleyard Lincoln. Harry Lincoln was well known for developing the Elysian range of craft. He built a large new factory on Babylon and a marina.

In 1966 he built a concrete bridge alongside the Waterside slipway to connect with Babylon, which is why the bridge is named Lincoln Bridge and not Babylon Bridge. Sadly, Appleyard Lincoln ran into financial problems in the 1970s, finally closing in 1975.

King's Ely opened a new boathouse in 1976–77 and a second marina was dug out in 1977. Both marinas are now privately owned by Jalsea Marine Services Ltd and are always full of boats, such is the popularity of boating along the Ouse and its tributaries.

15. Ely High Bridge

From early times there was a causeway to cross the fens between Stuntney and Ely. Bishop Hervey (1109–1133) is credited with building the first causeway, although there were probably much earlier causeways dating back to the Bronze Age. The causeway was often in a poor state and boats had to be used to take travellers from Stuntney's island onto Ely's island. Bishop Fordham's survey of 1417 starts at the High Bridge and mentions the Bridgemead, the field next to the bridge which provided part of the income for the bridge reeve to maintain the bridge on behalf of the Bishop.

References to a bridge can be confusing as there was a stone bridge that crossed the Cawdle Fen stream near Castlehythe, an area referred to in ancient surveys as Stonbrigge or Castelbrigge, but whatever wooden structure had been in place over the Ouse was replaced in 1833 by a new bridge. In 1909 this was replaced by a cast-iron bridge and this in turn by a three span concrete bridge in 1981, which is practical rather than attractive.

The bridge carries the busy A142 and takes traffic into Ely to one of the most-struck railway underpasses in the country. At the time of writing a long-awaited bypass with a new bridge to span the river and railway is being constructed to carry the A142 and leave the High Bridge to deal with purely local traffic.

Ely High Bridge.

16. An Ancient Market Town

Ely's economic importance to the surrounding fenland villages is as a market town. Ely's market dates from the thirteenth century and was held on the Market Hill, which was just outside the boundaries of the monastery on one of the highest points of the city.

Fish, meat, produce and livestock would probably have made up most of the early market sales. Goods could be conveyed by water, but after the creation of the turnpike roads at the end of the eighteenth century they were increasingly brought by road.

Ely Market.

The Bishop appointed a Clerk of the Market to collect the various tolls and supervise what was being sold and take any rogue traders before the Bishop's manorial court.

In 1801 the Market Day was moved from Saturday to Thursday.

Once the Bishop had lost his secular power in 1836, the management of the market was less than satisfactory and by the beginning of the twentieth century the market was struggling financially.

In 1918 the City of Ely Urban District Council purchased the market rights from the ecclesiastical commissioners. In 1974 East Cambridgeshire District Council took over responsibility for the market and expanded the markets to offer a Saturday Craft Market and then a Saturday Farmers' Market, and even a small Sunday Market. As well as the traditional traders, some of whom have been trading for over fifty years, there are now specialist continental markets and much more food on offer, bringing a wider clientele to what are traditionally Ely's busiest days.

The markets are now managed by a separate trading company of the District Council.

17. Ely Fairs

For a cathedral, being granted a fair charter was an economic blessing. Bishop Hervey was granted the first one in 1109 for a three-day fair linked to the vigil of St John the Baptist, which was 23 June and coincided with the Feast of St Etheldreda. In the fourteenth century two more fair charters were granted, one around Ascentiontide for twenty-two days, known as the 'new fair', and one of seventeen days around the Feast of St Lambert.

Fairs meant trade and this included everything from spices from the East, sugar, currants, figs, dates, incense, wax and tallow to furs and material, while Ely was well known for exporting its ale. Trade brought tolls for the cathedral and the fairs brought visitors and pilgrims to the shrine of St Etheldreda. In fact, St Ethledreda's fair introduced a new word into the English language. Etheldreda was known as St Audrey and cheap pieces of fairground merchandise were known as St Audrey's, and from that the word 'tawdry' entered common usage.

By the nineteenth century the fairs were concentrated on a May fair and an October fair both of which went on for nearly a fortnight. For many of the leading citizens of the city they were not popular, as they disrupted normal business and attracted rogues and vagabonds, tricksters and pickpockets, and encouraged rowdy behaviour fuelled by Ely's numerous public houses. In 1874 the fairs were reduced to three days each and were largely associated with entertainment.

The fairs, for many years associated with the Thurston family, took over the Market Place, but when the whole area was resurfaced with red brick paviors in 1994, leading to locals to dub it 'Red Square', the funfairs were moved to the Broad Street car park. The October fair ended in 1998 and there has been no May fair since 2014, so it looks as if Ely's long fair tradition has ended.

October Fair in 1978.

May Fair, *c.* 2000.

18. St Mary's Church

St Mary's Church was one of two parish churches, the other being Holy Trinity. It is an elegant and light building dating from the time of Bishop Eustace (1197–1215) and it is likely it was a rebuilding of an original church about which little is known, but quite probably it was considerably earlier than the cathedral itself.

When Ely had a monastery the Sacrist was responsible for St Mary's and appointed the curates to take the services. After the dissolution of the monastery the Dean and Chapter nominated the vicar.

The graveyard that surrounded the church was once the scene of activities by notorious resurrectionists. By the first half of the nineteenth century churchyards like St Mary's were getting full and new burials were sometimes quite shallow, and it was easy to reach the corpse digging quietly at night with wooden shovels. Charles Fowler and Johnson Smith of Cambridge made money by digging up recently buried bodies to supply them to anatomy schools. In December 1830, the body of Rebecca Stearman was found in a hamper at Marsh and William Swan's coach office. The local 'Burke and Hare' were arrested, tried and received twelve months' hard labour for their efforts.

St Mary's Church viewed from the West Tower of Ely Cathedral.

So concerned were relatives of the recently deceased that they would keep vigil in the churchyard, but the passing of the Anatomy Act of 1832 saw the macabre trade decline and eventually die out. St Mary's churchyard ceased to be used for burials in 1855.

The church itself was extensively renovated in 1876, when it was reroofed, the seats replaced and wooden galleries removed.

The ancient churchyard is now a well-maintained garden of rest and in 1985 an elegant and practical extension was built at the south side, providing a splendid function room with office space and toilets.

19. St John's Farm

At St John's Farm, which has been in the ownership of the Runciman family since 1925, are the remains of the Hospitals of St John and Mary Magdalen, which lay alongside one of the main routes into and out of the old town from the south. Although we know little of their origins, we do know that in 1240 Bishop Hugh de Northwold united the two hospitals and placed them under the control of the Sacrist of Ely. In Bentham's *History and Antiquities of the Conventual and Cathedral Church of Ely*, published in 1771, he writes: 'The Hospital

St John's Farm.

was to consist of thirteen Chaplains and Brethren, who were to have a common refectory and dormitory and wear a uniform habit.'

In the sixteenth century, along with part of the area around it and several other properties in the city, the estate was transferred to the ownership of Clare Hall, Cambridge. Clare Cottages on St John's Road relate to this ownership. Since that time the hospital remains have been part of a private farm.

20. The Old Palace

The Bishops of Ely had many palaces. The Old Palace in front of the West End of the cathedral is essentially the one built by Bishop John Alcock, who was Bishop from 1486–1500. The building has undergone many changes, with some parts lost after the Reformation. One of the features of the building is the long gallery, which runs alongside Palace Green and was built by Bishop Goodrich in 1549–50. After the death of Bishop Cox in 1581, the see was left vacant and the monarch collected the revenues for the Crown, and the palace was put to good use as a prison. It was in this long gallery that prominent Roman Catholics interred by Queen Elizabeth I between 1587 and 1600 took their exercise.

The Old Bishop's Palace.

The ancient plane tree.

The detention together of such prominent figures in the relative isolation of the island of Ely was probably not such a great idea and may well have contributed to the Gunpowder Plot of 1605, which involved some family members of those at Ely.

It was Bishop Laney, who was Bishop from 1667–75, who did much to restore the palace after years of neglect and convert it into a fine but more manageable residence.

The lovely walled gardens have a pond and nearby is one of the largest London plane trees in England, believed to have been planted in the time of Bishop Gunning (between 1675 and 1684). In 2002 the Tree Council, in celebration of Queen Elizabeth's Golden Jubilee, designated the London Plane of Ely as one of their fifty Great British Trees.

The palace was used by the Bishops of Ely until the early part of the Second World War when, in 1941, Bishop Wynn moved to the smaller old Deanery, now the Bishop's House, and the palace became a Red Cross and St John Ambulance home for convalescing servicemen. In 1946 the British Red Cross leased the palace as a school for disabled girls of secondary school age. In 1977 this became of co-educational school until closing in 1983, when it was taken over by the Sue Ryder charity as a residential home. This in turn closed in 2012.

The building has been given its new lease of life by King's Ely, with an extensive renovation as a Sixth Form Centre officially opened on 28 September 2012 by HRH Katharine, Duchess of Kent.

21. Palace Green

Le Grene was a large open space in front of the West End of the cathedral on which Bishop Hugh de Northwold built a chantry in 1250. In the eighteenth century the present splendid townhouse was built on the site.

Palace Green was the chosen setting for an extraordinary gift. In 1860 the Ely Volunteer Rifle Corps was founded and that same year, with much ceremony, Ely received the gift of a captured Russian cannon from the Siege of Sevastopol in the Crimean War. The cannon was conveyed by rail and arrived in the town accompanied by the Band of the Grenadier Guards, (not the Coldstream Guards, as had been expected). The cannon was hauled along Broad Street, up Fore Hill and down the High Street, and placed with great difficulty (as it kept sinking into the wet grass) onto the prepared stone base on Palace Green.

Not everyone approved of having a military object in such a prominent position in front of the cathedral, and some locals were keen to tell anyone who would listen that it was the same cannon that Cromwell had used to knock down the North West transept of the cathedral.

During the Second World War, the city authorities had to fight to keep the cannon lest it should be taken on one of the scrap metal drives.

Palace Green holds many secrets. One, commemorated by a plaque on a nearby wall, was that it was once the scene of a martyrdom. The short reign of Mary I between 1553 and

The Chantry.

The cannon on the Green outside Ely Cathedral.

1558 was a dangerous time for protestants. In 1555 William Wolsey of Upwell and Robert Pygot of Wisbech were accused of heresy and imprisoned at Ely. The Bishop of Ely, who had secular power over the see, had a prison on Gaol Lane, now known as Barton Road, possibly on the site where the Theological College was built.

They faced trial on 9 October 1555 and, refusing to recant their belief that the sacrament was not the natural body and blood of Christ, were found guilty and one week later were burned at the stake on Palace Green. It was the same day that Bishops Latimer and Ridley were similarly put to death at Oxford.

22. 'Heal the Sick'

The Chantry house was owned by several of Ely's most distinguished families, notably the Waddingtons. In 1846 the estate was sold and bought by the Muriel family, who were Ely doctors. It seems after this the rear of the estate became the southern side of St Mary's Street and developed with Waddington Terrace and other fine buildings.

Dr John Muriel, a surgeon, not only built Cathedral House for his son but also gave a plot of land on St Mary's Street for the building of a Dispensary. Opened in 1865, the doorway carries the inscription 'Heal the Sick'. Most poor people could not afford medical care and relied on the cures and potions recommended by elderly neighbours or 'wise women'. The fens were notoriously damp, misty and unhealthy and even in towns like Ely many lived in unsanitary and overcrowded cottages, using water taken from the river. Illnesses were treated with laudanum, a potent mixture of opium and alcohol, and opium

The Dispensary.

itself. There was a well known rhyme: 'Poppy tea and opium pill, Are the cure for many an ill.' The high dependency on opium was blamed for the fenman's seeming slowness of thought and feeblemindedness.

The provision of a Dispensary, like Dean Peacock's drive to build proper sewers and bring drinkable water to the city, can be seen as a further attempt to improve the health of the city's inhabitants. (The Public Health Board was established in 1850, with Dr John Muriel being one of the first members.)

The Ely and District Nursing Association, founded in 1886, became based at the Dispensary. There is a plaque on the wall commemorating Nurse Clarke, who served the people of Ely from 1907 to 1939, recording her remarkable dedication as District Nurse and as the British Red Cross Commandant in Ely during the Second World War.

After a Health Centre was built in Chapel Street in 1970, the Dispensary has had a number of uses, principally as a meeting place.

23. Prior Crauden's Chapel

One of Ely's secret treasures, Prior Crauden's Chapel, was nearly lost. John de Crauden was elected Prior in May 1321, shortly after John Hotham, who had been Chancellor of England, became Bishop. Along with Alan of Walsingham they were faced with an enormous challenge when, in February 1322, the central Norman tower of the cathedral collapsed. This was soon after work had begun on the Lady Chapel. Not only did the three

Prior Crauden's Chapel.

The interior of Prior Crauden's Chapel.

men work together to construct Ely's crowning glory – the octagonal lantern tower – and the wonderfully spacious Lady Chapel, but between 1322 and 1328 Prior Crauden built a lovely two-storey chapel beside the Prior's House, which he also extended with a new hall and study.

Once adorned with stained-glass windows, which were presumably destroyed during the zealous Bishop Goodrich's time in office (1534–1555), at the Dissolution of the monastery in 1538 it could have been sold just for the building materials but was converted into a private house. From about 1846 it was restored as much as possible to its original condition as a chapel and used by King's Ely.

In 1986 the chapel was restored with funding from English Heritage, King's Ely and The Pilgrim Trust. A key can be obtained from the cathedral to allow access to the building, but note that the chapel is reached by a steep and narrow winding staircase.

24. What Are the Two High Street Gates?

The High Street was once known as Steeple Row, a name now transferred to the walk behind the High Street buildings. Steeple Gate was the entrance to the churchyard of Holy Trinity and the church of St Cross. The gate dates back to before 1417 and is built over an earlier undercroft. It was restored in 1978 and became a tea room.

Left: Steeple Gate.

Right: Sacrist's Gate.

Ely's second parish church and much the larger of the two, Holy Trinity, was centred on the cathedral and worship took place in the cathedral nave. As with St Mary's it was under the jurisdiction of the Sacrist, who appointed the chaplain to conduct the worship. While the monastery was in existence the services of the monks interrupted those of St Cross and the parishioners asked for a church of their own. During the time of Bishop Langham (Bishop from 1362–66) a new parochial church of St Cross was completed. Dedicated to the Holy Trinity, the church was a 'lean-to' structure against the north side of the nave, with an entrance from the north transept. It was poorly lit and ventilated and unpopular with the worshippers. It survived for 200 years before it was demolished in 1566 and the parishioners were given the daytime use of the Lady Chapel as their church of Holy Trinity.

Holy Trinity churchyard was cleared of its tombstones in 1962 and laid out as Cross Green, a popular space for informal leisure or cathedral events.

The other gateway on the north side of the cathedral, connecting the city with the monastery and Cathedral College, is the Sacrist's Gate. It is in a range of medieval buildings, now mostly converted into shops, including the Goldsmith's tower, built in 1325–26 by Alan of Walsingham, probably the most famous sacrist in the history of the cathedral. It was Alan of Walsingham who masterminded the construction of the octagonal lantern tower after the original Norman tower collapsed in 1321.

From 1858–1947 the Cathedral Choir school occupied part of the range alongside the gate. In 1974 Ely Museum began in the same premises until moving to the Bishop's Gaol in 1997. Octagon Dance Studio now uses the building.

25. Oliver Cromwell's House

Ely's most controversial resident was Oliver Cromwell. Cromwell and his family moved into the house in 1636 when he inherited the position of 'Farmer of the Tithes' from his maternal uncle, Sir Thomas Steward of Stuntney Hall, who had died childless. He had to see that the tithes were collected and pay a fixed sum of money to provide five quarters (a quarter was two stones in weight) of wheat twice yearly, also straw and a boar annually to the Dean and Chapter. He was also responsible for paying the chaplains at St Mary's and Holy Trinity Church and maintaining the chancel of St Mary's, but there was sufficient income over for the family to live well and his wife, Elizabeth, was well known for her prudent housekeeping. In 1988 East Cambridgeshire District Council bought the house that had been the vicarage for St Mary's Church and in 1990 opened it as a visitor attraction and Tourist Information Centre.

Oliver Cromwell's House.

Re-enactors outside Oliver Cromwell's House in 2017.

The house the Cromwells moved into dates from the thirteenth century and the parlour and kitchen are very much as the family would have known them. The house often hosts period re-enactors and visitors can learn from 'Poor Joan' – as royalists dubbed Elizabeth Cromwell – even take away her recipe for eel pie.

After the Cromwells left Ely in 1647, the lease was held by various tenants until Jonathan Page, who was last farmer of the tithes in 1836. In 1843 Joseph Rushbrook brought the house and turned it into the Cromwell Arms. Rushbrook put the house and small brewery up for sale in 1869, but it didn't sell and he became bankrupt. It passed through other hands until 1905, when the Revd Elgood Punchard, vicar of St Mary's, bought it and it became the vicarage.

26. Did Oliver Cromwell Vandalise the Cathedral?

Cromwell was blamed by many for knocking down the missing North West Transept (in fact it fell down towards the end of the fifteenth century, although there are those who believe it may not have been fully completed anyway) and destroying the Lady Chapel sculptures, which was done on the orders of Bishop Goodrich during the Reformation. He was also accused of stabling his horses in the Galilee Porch, which he may have done.

West front of Ely Cathedral from
Palace Green.

DID YOU KNOW?

The cathedral was surveyed in 1648 and found to be in a 'ruinous condition' and
when Parliament abolished Deans, chapters and cathedrals in 1649, the fate of the
cathedral hung in the balance. It might have been saved because the Lady Chapel
was the Holy Trinity Church, or it might have been because the monastic buildings
housed the King's School founded by royal charter in 1541; most likely, though, it
wasn't demolished because there was no profit in it.

27. Stories in Stained Glass

The zeal with which the Reformation affected the cathedral led to statues being defaced,
notably in the Lady Chapel and other small chapels, and stained glass being smashed.
Most of the stained glass that can be seen in the cathedral was installed during the great
Victorian restoration under the direction of Dean Peacock, firstly assisted by his Cambridge
University friend Professor Robert Willis and after 1847 by George Gilbert Scott.

Many of the windows were given as gifts and began at the east end in 1837 and continued for thirty years, driven by Canon Edward Sparke, son of Bowyer Edward Sparke, Bishop of Ely from 1812–1836. One of the newer windows installed in 1955 is the Royal Air Force memorial window. During the Second World War Ely was surrounded by aerodromes, most of them bomber command stations. The depiction in stained glass of a Wellington bomber flying over the cathedral is a poignant reminder of how airmen used the cathedral as a landmark.

One of the great delights of the cathedral is The Stained Glass Museum. This is a national collection and there are beautiful examples on display, from medieval to modern. The museum also stages workshops, activities and talks. To fully enjoy the collection it is necessary to be able to climb a stone spiral staircase of forty steps, but there is a touchscreen virtual tour available on the ground floor.

IN HONOUR AND MEMORY OF THE

The Bomber Command memorial window at Ely Cathedral.

The Stained Glass Museum, Ely. (© The Stained Glass Museum)

28. The Remarkable Mr Bentham

James Bentham was a remarkable man. He was born into a clerical family, the son of Revd Samuel Bentham, a canon of Ely Cathedral and vicar of Witchford. He was educated at King's Ely and then Trinity College, Cambridge, gaining a BA. He became a canon at Ely in 1737 and held a number of livings, mainly in Norfolk.

He is remembered mostly for his monumental historical work *The History and Antiquities of the Conventual Church of Ely*, which he began working on in 1756 and was published in 1771. He was also involved in more practical acts that had a great impact on the lives of local people. He proposed draining Grunty Fen, which did not happen at the time, but in 1757 he proposed a scheme for turnpike roads and eventually, with the support of Bishop Mawson, the Cambridge and Ely Turnpike Trust was established through an Act of Parliament passed in 1763. This entailed building a new bridge over the Old West River at Stretham Ferry.

Some of the gravel for the road came from Barton Fields, which accounts for many of the dips and hollows. The turnpike road was taken from Ely to Soham and then Ely to Sutton and Ely to Littleport. Later these roads were extended, with the Littleport road taken on to Downham Market. Turnpike Trusts collected tolls from travellers and were responsible for maintaining the roads. The paying of tolls died out towards the end of the nineteenth century, when the new county councils became responsible for the roads.

To mark his 70th birthday in 1779, James Bentham planted an avenue of oak trees on Lynn Road at the entrance to the city. An obelisk, now in a private garden, commemorates this with the words 'May this benefit the next generation.' His son completed the planting in 1787 and some of the oaks survive today. James Bentham died in 1794 at the age of 86, but he is remembered in Bentham Way, off Kings Avenue.

Left: Turnpike marker on Witchford Road.

Below: James Bentham's monument at the Oakery.

29. A Lasting Legacy

In 1730 Mrs Catherine Needham died at New Alresford in Hampshire. She was the widow of the Revd William Venn Needham and he had left her well provided for with property in Ely. At her death she owned the White Hart Inn and the extensive land behind it, land in Newnham Street, the house of Mr Legge the brewer on Market Street, and other property.

In her will she left most of her fortune to build a school in Ely for the education of poor boys. This would be governed and maintained by a trust in her name that would also manage the income from the estates.

A site was found for a new school building on Back Hill, backing onto the Park. In 1742 the school opened for twenty-four poor boys, who were each given a school uniform of hat, green tailcoat with brass buttons, white corduroy knee breeches, shirt and shoes. William Cawthorne was appointed the first schoolmaster and a house was built for him alongside the school.

While the school building still stands with a plaque above what was the main entrance, nothing remains of the house. This charity school grew into Needham's School, the secondary modern school for Ely, which eventually moved to new premises on Downham Road in 1968, while the old building is leased by King's Ely.

The school that grew from the original bequest is now the City of Ely College, but Needham's Charity Trustees continue to meet to assist in the education of young people in Ely today. In 2016 the Sixth Form College that shares the Downham Road site changed its name to Bishop Laney College after another benefactor of local education, Bishop Benjamin Laney (1667–1675), whose charity is also still active today.

Former Needham's School, Back Hill.

30. Who Was Thomas Parsons?

Like Catherine Needham, Thomas Parsons was a benefactor of the City of Ely, although very little is known about him. The Ely historian, the late Reg Holmes, carried out extensive research and found various different references and spellings which might relate to Thomas Parsons in the fifteenth century, but all that can be said is that when he died that century he bequeathed to certain feoffees land, tenements, and fisheries at Stretham to pay property taxes levied by Parliament for the use of the monarch.

In the sixteenth century the feoffees of the charity began to acquire property in Ely and by the seventeenth century the terms of the charity were changed to helping the poor of Ely. Some of the most powerful people in Ely became governors of the charity and Oliver Cromwell was one such governor while he was in Ely.

In the early 1840s George Basevi, one of the leading church architects of his day, designed an open courtyard of almshouses on St Mary's Street for Parsons Charity, to replace some Broad Street almshouses that were in poor repair. This was on the site of Sextry Barn, which had been one of the largest medieval tithe barns in Europe. Basevi was the uncle of Benjamin Disraeli and perhaps better known for designing the Fitzwilliam Museum in Cambridge, but unfortunately he did not live to see the almshouses finished, for while he was inspecting building work high up on scaffolding inside the West Tower of the cathedral in 1845, he fell through a hole in the scaffolding to his death. His almshouses, now renamed Thomas Parsons Square, still provide homes in Ely.

Thomas Parsons Square.

The charity has built other accommodation in Ely, notably Bamford House in Deacons Lane in 1976, named after the widely respected Ely general practitioner Dr Brian Bamford, High Sheriff between 1964 and 1965.

31. Highflyer

In days gone by many local people would confidently assert that James Bentham's obelisk at the Oakery was a monument to the famous racehorse Highflyer. Highflyer also gave his name to the Newnham Street public house which has been serving the people of Ely since the 1790s.

Highflyer was one of the most famous racehorses of his day and in 1779 he was bought by Richard Tattersall. Tattersall had set up a horse auction near Hyde Park Corner in London in 1766. He was a very wealthy man and knew everyone in the horseracing world.

Tattersall already leased 60 acres of land at New Barns estate to the north of Ely and he put Highflyer out to stud there, making a fortune; in fact, he was criticised for overbreeding him, but he did produce 469 winners including three derby winners, three St Leger winners and an Epsom Oaks winner. Tattersall built Highflyer Hall for his country home, at which he entertained many famous guests including the future King George IV.

When Highflyer died in 1793, the horse was buried in front of the bay windows of the house. The Tattersall name lives on in Tattersall's sale ring at Newmarket. Richard Tattersall, 'Old Tatt' as he was known, died in 1796 and for a short while his business at Ely passed to his son, Edmund, 'Young Tatt', but by about 1802 he had left Ely.

Highflyer Hall.

For a while Marengo (*c.* 1793–1831), Napoleon's horse captured at Waterloo in 1815, was put to stud at Highflyer Hall by Lt-Col Angerstein of the Grenadier Guards. Marengo is not buried at the farm – his skeleton, minus a hoof which was turned into a snuffbox, is at the National Army Museum in Chelsea.

Highflyer Hall is part of P.J. Lee's family farming business of over 6,000 acres and the private home of Richard Lee and his family, who specialise in growing potatoes for the chip shop industry.

32. The Fen Office

Before the seventeenth-century drainage, the fens around Ely were marsh and swamp, with slow-flowing rivers and large meres or lakes. There was some summer grazing, but much of the fenland was the haunt of fishermen and wildfowlers.

The work of the seventeenth-century drainage engineers, principally Sir Cornelius Vermuyden in the 1650s, largely funded by the Duke of Bedford and the Company of Adventurers, transformed the landscape so that they could make money from farming the land.

In 1663 the Bedford Level Corporation was established to maintain the drainage, effectively replacing the old Commissioners of Sewers.

In 1844 the Corporation established a grand Ely office by purchasing Bedford House on St Mary's Street. Samuel Wells was the Registrar of the Bedford Corporation and he

The Fen Office.

moved into the house with his wife, Sarah Ann. Chatteris-born Wells was a radical lawyer and became the registrar in 1824. In 1830 he wrote *A History of the Drainage of the Bedford Level* and the same year he attacked the wealth of Bishop Sparke of Ely, and particularly the patronage he extended to his own family by giving them the livings of various parishes.

Later members of the Archer family, the Ely Solicitors, held the post of registrar through Thomas to Goodwyn and finally to Harold Archer.

In 1864 the Corporation sold the main house and moved to the single-storey section with its splendid coat of arms above the door carrying the motto *Arridet Aridum*, translated as 'Dryness is Pleasing', or words to that effect.

In 1920 the Ouse Drainage Board took over the responsibilities of the Corporation. This lasted until 1930, before becoming part of the River Great Ouse Catchment Board until 1952, and then eventually Anglian Water before the building was sold to Cambridgeshire County Council in 1968.

From the late 1980s the Fen Office has been part of the Bedford House day centre complex, but the splendid crest remains above the door as a reminder of its history.

33. Market Street Infants' School

In 2016 the Isle of Ely Primary School was officially opened in north Ely. It is spacious, with outdoor learning areas and a large playing field. How different from Ely's first Victorian schools, which have all been demolished with the exception of Market Street Infants'

Former Market Street Infants' School.

School. The school was built in 1820 on the site of the old bridewell to take girls from the Market Place Sessions House, where they had been upstairs. The Sessions House had been replaced with a new building on the Lynn Road and the new school was behind it on Market Street. It was a small schoolroom and the building was enlarged in 1868 as a mixed infants' school. By that date there were two National Schools, at Broad Street and Silver Street.

The Market Street school was L-shaped with large rooms that were divided into about three teaching areas, with a small hard-surfaced enclosed play area.

The school closed in 1953 when long-serving Headmistress Miss Hazel retired after thirty-two years and a new school was opened on Downham Road called St Audrey's. St Audrey's was in turn replaced by Spring Meadow School at High Barns, with the old St Audrey's after a time becoming a Sixth Form Centre, now being Highfield Special School.

The former Market Street school has been Pettit's second-hand furniture shop, then for a short while an Indian restaurant. Under the ownership of East Cambridgeshire District Council the building was renovated, creating a second floor, and from 1997 until 2015 it was the offices of the City of Ely Council with the council chamber above.

Today the building is used partly by ACRE, the Registrar's Office, and the Citizens Advice Bureau.

34. The Bishop's Gaol

The maintenance of law and order and the punishment of wrongdoing was effectively in the hands of the Church in Ely. The Bishop of Ely had secular powers over the Liberty of Ely until 1836. He appointed the clergy, many of whom were also magistrates. There are references to the Bishop's Gaol dating back to the thirteenth century, when it seems to have been on Barton Road, known for many years as Gaol Lane, probably where the Theological College was built. It is recorded as having been demolished in 1852.

The Bishop's Gaol that most people are familiar with is today Ely Museum. It was Bishop Gunning (1674–86) who replaced the old gaol by buying a large private house around 1679 on the corner of High Row (later Gaol Street and now Market Street) and Lynn Road. Various reports say that it was in a poor condition and prisoners often escaped, so much so that in Bishop Mawson's time (1754–1771) prisoners were routinely chained to the floor. As in the House of Correction, there were iron bars across the floor so that prisoners could be manacled to them. One particularly gruesome form of punishment was an iron collar with spikes that was placed around the prisoner's neck so that he could not rest his head. As in the bridewell or House of Correction the prisoners could pay the gaoler so they might receive slightly better conditions, like a bed to sleep on rather than straw.

In 1836, when the Liberty of Ely was abolished and the secular jurisdiction of the Bishop of Ely ended, the gaol closed. Benjamin Barlow, who had been in charge of the House of Correction, had been the gaoler for thirty-four years, and at one time managing both buildings.

The building was sold and soon became the home of Marshall Fisher, clerk to Ely lawyer William Marshall. A man of learning, he established Ely Mechanic's Institute there in 1842, with a library of almost 2,000 volumes. In 1849 he set up a small museum. Fisher died in 1899 at the age of 92 and in 1904 the Bishop bought the building and used it to store Diocesan records.

From October 1973 the building became part of the new East Cambridgeshire District Council and the City of Ely Council had its chamber and office on the first floor. In 1995 the City Council moved into new offices and a new council chamber in the old Market Street Infants' School building, and with East Cambridgeshire District Council's leaving the building and the Registrar for Births and Deaths moving to the rear of the old school building opposite, the way was clear for Ely Museum to move in, which they did, and Ely Museum was officially opened by Michael Petty MBE, MA (Cantab), ALA on 26 April 1997. Needless to say, the old cells form an important part of Ely's history in a museum which has introduced thousands of children to living history.

A cell at Ely Museum.

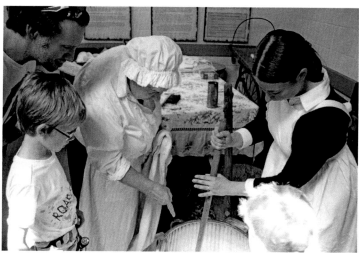

A Victorian 'washing machine' being demonstrated.

35. A Grim History

The Bishop's Gaol played a significant role in one of the most lamentable times in Ely's long history, the Ely and Littleport Riots of 1816.

The men of Littleport, desperate to be able to afford food for their families after failed harvests, rioted in the village on 22 May and then marched on Ely. Sadly, having been granted their demands, they went on something of a drunken rampage, joined by some of the rougher elements of Ely.

They came to trial in the Sessions House on Ely's Market Place. The authorities – Edward Christian, Chief Justice of the Isle, along with Mr Justice Abbot and Mr Justice Burrough – were determined to make examples of them. There was a fear in the country that there might be a revolution, as there had been in France some thirty or so years before. Twenty-four men were sentenced to death, but in the event nineteen had their sentences reduced to imprisonment or deportation, leaving five men to remain in the Bishop's Gaol awaiting their fate.

On Friday 28 June 1816 William Beamiss, George Crow, John Dennis, Isaac Harley and Thomas South were conveyed through the streets of Ely to somewhere near the old chalk pits, known as Parnell Pits or sometimes Mill Pits, as there was once a windmill along St John's Road nearby. This was the site of the gallows and it was here that the five men from Littleport were hanged in front of hundreds of people who had come to watch. They were then buried in St Mary's churchyard, where there is a plaque recording their names and the inscription, 'May their awful fate be a warning to others'.

St John's Road Playing Field.

Housing spread along St John's Road with the building of Debden Green in 1948, and the old pits area was eventually transformed into a popular and well-used play area with Ely's skate park. After many years of fundraising, the edge of the playing field is also home to the Scout Hut and the Guide Hut.

36. The Sessions House

The old Sessions House on the Market Place was not really large enough to manage a huge trial like that of the Ely and Littleport rioters. It was certainly not grand enough for Edward Christian, Chief Justice of the Isle and the older brother of Fletcher Christian, who led the mutiny aboard the *Bounty* in 1789 and died on the Pitcairn Islands in 1793.

Four years after that trial, work was begun on a magnificent new courthouse on the Lynn Road, on land just north of the Bishop's Gaol. The new building was at the instigation of the Bishop of Ely, Bowyer Edward Sparke. It would have behind it a new House of Correction to replace the old bridewell. This was a statement of authority to the ignorant fenmen and women who would have the misfortune to be brought here.

On Tuesday 26 February 1822 Lord Chief Justice Christian conducted his first assize in the new building, remarking at the time on its elegance and beauty and the commodious arrangements which had been made for facilitating public business.

The Sessions House.

The first major trial in the Sessions House was that of John Rolfe, found guilty of murdering a fellow poacher, probably to rob him of his few possessions. Judge Christian, passing sentence in February 1823, declared: 'You are unfit for earth, unworthy of heaven and are sentenced to be hanged by the neck until you are dead.' After the unfortunate Rolfe was hanged his body was covered in pitch, placed in hoops and suspended on a gibbet in Padnal Fen, in view of his father's house. For many years he swung there as a grisly warning and gruesome attraction for the curious. The vain Justice Christian died a few weeks later, in, as one of his contemporaries sneered, 'the full vigour of his incapacity'.

The Sessions House, or Shire Building, was not just a court but also a large meeting place. In the north wing was the armoury for the 6th Cambridgeshire Rifles, while the south wing contained a chapel for the House of Correction. In 1843 this wing became Ely's police station, before they moved into new premises on the corner of Nutholt Lane and Lynn Road in 1970.

The Court Service closed the courts in 2011, making the building redundant. Understandably there was much concern locally, first at the loss of the court, then at the possible loss of the listed building. However, in 2013 the City of Ely Council bought the building for the community at a cost of £1. Having moved the council offices into the north wing, the council is currently developing the building for community use.

Listed interior of the Sessions House.

37. The House of Correction

The police station moved into the south wing of the Sessions House in 1843 while a new House of Correction with thirty-five cells was being built.

The new House of Correction was the work of George Basevi, who also designed Thomas Parsons Square, the two projects going on simultaneously.

According to Robert Gardner in his *Historical Gazeteer of Cambridgeshire*, published in 1850, the number of prisoners in the House of Correction in 1849 averaged ninety-one, a considerable increase on an average of sixty-six in 1848. He noted that 'the tread wheel and oakum picking are the usual modes of punishment and the house of correction was run on the silent or Pentonville system.'

It was not in existence for long as the Prisons Act of 1877 took the responsibility for prisons away from local control and put them under the authority of the Home Secretary, as a result of which the House of Correction was closed in 1878.

There are references to a subterranean passage from the House of Correction to the Session's House, but this has yet to be confirmed with any physical evidence.

The site of the House of Correction was then purchased by Ebenezer William Harlock in 1880 for a private house, and The Grange was built on the site.

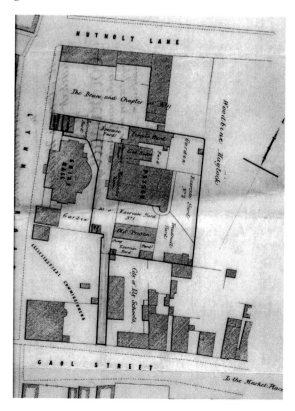

House of Correction sale plan from 1880.

38. Tower Hospital

Under the Poor Law Act of 1815, the parish was responsible for the welfare of the poor. In Ely, as there were two parishes, there were two parish workhouses. St Mary's workhouse was on St Mary's Street on the site of what became the Plough and Fleece and then the Kum In Cafe, while Holy Trinity workhouse was at the foot of Fore Hill and was later swallowed up by the Fore Hill brewery. Churchwardens who had the ability to help poor families were powerful figures in their communities.

The Poor Law Amendment Act of 1834 led to the building of workhouses, where anyone needing help had to enter the workhouse in order to receive it. In Ely a large area of land was purchased at the top of Cambridge Road and plans were drawn up for a building to cater for not just the two Ely parishes but a union of parishes, which included Coveney, Little Downham, Grunty Fen, Haddenham, Wilburton, Littleport, Mepal, Sutton, Wentworth, Witchford, Little Thetford and Stretham. A Board of Guardians was elected and Ely solicitor William Marshall Jnr was appointed clerk.

Tower Court.

The Union Workhouse was opened in 1837. It could accommodate 340 people, with men and women kept separately, and married couples only having the chance to meet at the compulsory Sunday chapel. The inmates were clothed and fed a basic diet, relying heavily on gruel, bread, soup, broth, vegetables and a little meat; this diet could be supplemented with a little ale for the over 60s if the medical officer considered it would improve their health.

The Union Workhouses were built approximately 15 miles apart, which was the distance a vagrant or 'gentleman of the road' could walk in a day. Other workhouses were at Newmarket, Cambridge and Downham Market. A popular term for the Union Workhouses was 'the Spike', possibly because one of the tasks given to the inmates was unpicking oakum on a spike.

After the introduction of the National Health Service in 1948 the workhouse became a home for the elderly and renamed the Tower Hospital, taking its name from the city water towers nearby. The old buildings were adapted and new lounges added, and a Friends Group was very active in raising money to support the care of patients there. In 1961 the Friends successfully revived the Hospital Sunday Parade and this was a successful fundraising event for many years. The hospital ceased to be used for the care of the elderly in 1993 and in 1998 the Springboard Housing Association converted some of the buildings and the chapel into Tower Court residential units.

39. Steam, Mighty Steam

In 1843 news came that the new railway system might come to Ely. The driving force behind the proposed railway line was Samuel Morton Peto, of the engineers Grissell and Peto. Peto had invested heavily in making Lowestoft a successful port and he needed to connect it to London, so he proposed a new line from Newport through Cambridge and Ely to Brandon in Suffolk and then on to Norwich.

Such railway proposals were sometimes met with opposition locally from landowners but in 1839 one of the most remarkable men in Ely's history had become Dean of the cathedral. George Peacock, a distinguished mathematician and Lowdean Professor of Astronomy at Cambridge University, not only faced the challenge of restoring the cathedral but was also determined to improve the health and economy of the town itself.

In January 1844 at the Sessions House, the Dean, along with former High Sheriff William Layton of Woodhouse, a leading farmer, and four Directors of the company were present to inform the meeting of the benefits of the new railway in transporting local produce and stock. In the short term the building of the railway meant well-paid jobs, compared with farm-work wages, and hundreds of local men benefitted.

In 1845, after a remarkable feat of Victorian engineering in constructing a railway across the fens, the station opened at Ely and soon there were connections not just to London and Norwich, but new lines to Kings Lynn and March onto Peterborough. Ely, the once isolated island city, had truly entered a new age.

Ely station.

40. River Trade

There was inevitably some opposition to the new railway from those who used the river system to transport goods, and on which Ely had relied so heavily for so many years. Fenland lighters traditionally worked the fenland waterways. A lighter was a long, narrow barge capable of carrying a heavy load, but able to work where there was not much depth of water. Lighters worked in gangs, usually of four, hauled by a horse who was led by a horse knocker boy, who walked along the haling way beside the river.

Some thought that the money spent on the railway could be better used on deepening the River Ouse north of Ely, as Ely was an important port for coal with Humber Keels, with cargoes of some 80 tons coming up the Ouse.

The answer was to build two docks at Ely. The first was close to the new station on the other side of the turnpike road, opposite Babylon and close to the railway bridge; the second was much larger, along Cawdle Fen, and took the barges under the railway into a new dock running back towards the station. The river trade continued to decline, however, and the advent of motor transport and an improved road network in the twentieth century saw the end of goods being transported by barge and the docks becoming redundant and filled in.

One of the last working boats seen on the Ouse was Ted Appleyard's *Shell Fen*, a dutch barge that was the smallest oil tanker in the Shell fleet and which had been on the Ouse since about 1912, firstly transporting bulbs and other produce and then fitted out for oil in 1939. *Shell Fen* was sold in 1970 and left the Ouse.

For many years the river at Ely lay dormant except for fishing, but then the leisure craft began to take over. Ely is so popular now that the council introduced time limits for mooring boats in 2016, so there are greater opportunities for visitors to be able to stay for twenty hours and see something of the city. In 2017, Ely's first hotel barge opened for business and there is a floating restaurant which, along with the other restaurants and Peacock's award-winning tearooms, makes the riverside a vibrant and busy place today.

Right: The *Shell Fen* barge.

Below: Moorings on the
River Ouse.

41. Cutter Inn

Before the railway arrived in Ely, there had been many attempts to improve the River Ouse for navigation from King's Lynn. One of the most significant was between 1827 and 1830, when a new straight section was cut from Queen Adelaide towards Littleport.

The effect was to bypass the big loop in the river that took it to Prickwillow, where it met the River Lark, leaving the old bed dry from near Turbotsey to Prickwillow. This stretch of the river had been notorious for the shingle ridge, which often grounded barges. It is said that the old Plough Inn which stood on this stretch of the river was partly built from blocks of stone bound for Ely that had to be taken off to lighten the barges.

There were great civic celebrations when the New Cut, or Sandys Cut, was opened, for not only would it improve navigation but it would also help to drain the Padnal area of the fens, so more of it could be brought into cultivation.

An added benefit for Ely was that two malsters' cottages at Quayside, next to an ancient brewery, were converted into a new public house – the Cutter. The old public house on Broad Street became the Cutter Tap. The Cutter, of course, took its name from those navvies who cut the river, not from the sailing vessel.

Of all the great many public houses that Ely had in the nineteenth century, the Cutter, which is as busy as ever, is one of only eight survivors.

The Cutter Inn.

42. Life on the River

Today the *Liberty Belle* runs regular pleasure trips from near the Maltings, navigating the river among the pleasure craft and the water bicycles and , of course, the wildlife.

In Edwardian times there were few pleasure craft. Men could supplement the family's meals with fresh river fish and there were fishing clubs like the one based at the Marquis of Granby pub, which was in Victoria Street. They had enjoyable trips on the *Pattie* and some competitions.

There was also a River Trip Society, which the ladies could enjoy as well, on the steam launch the *Nancy*, which usually plied its trade carrying cargo between Kings Lynn and Cambridge. The electric launch, the *Viscountess Bury*, was also a popular site on the Cam and the Ouse.

Ely can boast the largest number of feral Muscovy ducks in the country. Not everyone likes them because of the mess, and steps have been taken in recent years to control their numbers. But how did they come to be a feature of the riverside? Local knowledge suggests that originally some were purchased at Ely market and instead of being kept in a farmyard, for which they are more suited, were released onto the riverside. They are prolific breeders and, for those who like them, great characters.

A fishing match setting out on the *Pattie* in July 1912. (Photo by Tom Bulton)

Above: Liberty Belle River Cruises.

Left: Muscovy duck with brood.

43. 'Backs Between Your Knees'

The Cambridge University boat crew has trained on the Ouse at Ely for many years. They used the boathouse, now Grand Central Restaurant, at Annesdale and then a King's Ely boathouse on Babylon, but in 2016 opened a brand new £5 million boathouse on the wash north of Ely for all the University crews, male and female.

In 1944 the Cambridge and Oxford University boat race was held on the River Ouse, on the straight cut opened in 1830 north of Queen Adelaide towards Littleport. In 2004, local men Jack Waterhouse and Terry Overall organised the Diamond 44 committee to commemorate the Diamond Jubilee of this unique wartime event. The commemoration included a challenge race between former Cambridge and Oxford blues along the same stretch of water and a film highlighting the other Ely connection with the boat race, that of the role of Dean Charles Merivale of Ely Cathedral, who was Dean from 1869 to 1894 and while a student at Cambridge was the leading blue protagonist in the challenge to Oxford for the first race in 1829.

King's Ely continues to be a strong rowing school and competes at national regattas.

A lasting legacy of Diamond 44 was the establishment of the Isle of Ely Rowing Club. The club, with a boathouse nearly opposite the University one, has been hugely successful in a short space of time, developing rowing talent young and old.

Dean Merrivale's memorial, Ely Cathedral.

The official opening of the University Boathouse, 3 December 2016.

44. The Corn Exchange

For a little under 120 years the Corn Exchange dominated the Market Hill. The railway had arrived in Ely and local farmers and businessmen were optimistic. Now was the time to clear away the old Sessions House and the clutter of buildings there and build an Exchange 'worthy of the wealth and importance of the district'.

In 1846 the 'Ely Fairs and Cattle Market and Corn Exchange' was formed and the creation of a cattle market and the building of a corn exchange got underway. Problems over delivering the stone delayed the Exchange until 1847, and when it did open it was not entirely favourably received, as many found it dark, so a new glass roof was installed by public subscription in 1854. There was a poultry market at the rear of the Exchange alongside the Butter Market, but this was not successful so in 1855 this was converted into a public reading room, then with the public room.

The Corn Exchange was more than just the place to do business on a Thursday; it was also Ely's largest public venue and over the years has played host to everything from a VE-Day dance in 1945, dinners and children's tea parties to boxing tournaments.

Gradually, however, the business of buying and selling corn declined. The Urban District Council wouldn't meet the asking price from the company and the building, along with the public room (Exchange Cinema), was sold to a London developer. In 1963 the site was cleared and a central block of shops replaced it – 'the monster by the minster,' as Ian Nairn of the *Observer* dubbed it.

Corn Exchange, *c.* 1910.

The 'Monster by the Minster', 2017.

DID YOU KNOW?

In 1940, after the evacuation of Dunkirk, some of the rescued Allied soldiers were accommodated at the Corn Exchange while in transit.

45. The Cemetery

In 1850 a report entitled 'Preliminary Inquiry into the Sewerage, Drainage and Supply of Water and Sanitary Conditions of the Inhabitants' by William Lee was published. The report was damning of the living conditions, absence of sanitation and lack of a clean water supply in Ely. Action followed and in 1850 the Local Board of Health was established, with Dean George Peacock as its Chairman. In 1853 the Dean laid the foundation stone of a new water tower at the top of Cambridge Road. At first water was drawn from the River Ouse and taken to filter beds near the Angel public house, but later a water supply was brought from boreholes at Isleham.

Clean water was followed by the laying of sewers to connect to a new works on the area now known as Lavender Green, next to the river.

Local solicitor William Marshall was appointed Clerk to the new Public Health Board and one of his early tasks was to find a site for a new cemetery. Six acres of land were purchased on the edge of the New Barns estate. J.P. Pritchett Jnr of Darlington designed two fine chapels – one for non-conformists and one for Anglicans – and the cemetery lodge for the curator. Richard Freeman, a highly respected local builder, was responsible for building them and the new cemetery opened in May 1855, managed by a burial board of fifteen elected members.

Ely cemetery.

The old mill mound.

The graves of Dean
George Peacock,
Canon William Selwyn
and Canon Edward
Bowler Sparke.

The cemetery was extended to take in land to the north and Mill Hill Close, which ran alongside Common Road. Legend has it that the mound that can be seen in the cemetery is the burial site of cholera victims, but of course it isn't; the cholera deaths may have given rise to the need for the cemetery but the mound is that of the windmill that once stood there.

Dean George Peacock, who did so much for the cathedral and for the city, died in 1858 and is buried in the cemetery, where he was joined by his brother-in-law, Canon William Selwyn, and Edward Bowler Sparke, in an area where several distinguished members of the cathedral chapter are interred.

The Burial Board finished in 1979 and the management and maintenance of the cemetery is now in the hands of the City of Ely Council. Although the South Chapel is used as a workshop, in 1999 the North Chapel was restored and is available for services. It is a fine small building with a very nice stained-glass window designed by Reginald Hallward in 1937.

46. Bona Cervisia

Ely had been a brewing town since monastic times. In 1319, fourteen of the Bishop's men were given safe conduct to sell ale at Lynn and Boston, while John Chamberleyn was allowed to export 200 barrels of ale, 'so long as he did not sell them to the Scots'. Beer was important as it was safer to drink than Ely water!

There were several small breweries in the town. In the nineteenth century there was T & H Legge's brewery on Market Street, while around 1850 William Scales built the Eagle and Lamb public house on Cambridge Road, with a small brewery behind it. In 1856 this was taken over by Richard Porter until it was sold to Morgan's brewery in 1879.

In the second half of the nineteenth century there were two major brewing families in Ely, the Harlocks and the Halls. In the 1850s William Harlock was living at Quay House and owned the Quay Brewery. The Hall family bought Marche's brewery at Waterside in 1700 and in 1871 built a new brewery at the foot of Fore Hill.

The brewers were figures of importance in the town. They lived in fine houses with domestic staff, and played a prominent role in civic affairs. In 1888 both Bertram Hall and Ebenezer Harlock were members of the Board of Health. They were also farmers, growing their own barley. They employed many people and built houses for their workers, which can be identified in some cases by stone plaques.

Labels from Ely Brewery.

In 1912 Frank Litchfield Harlock joined companies with William Cutlack of Littleport to form Cutlack & Harlock Ltd at the Quay Brewery, which was enlarged. Cutlack & Harlock then took over Legge's Brewery and Percy Brewery of Soham.

In 1930 came the major amalgamation of A & B Hall and Cutlack & Harlock to form Hall, Cutlack & Harlock Ltd, based at the Forehill Brewery, with the Quayside Brewery switching to mineral water production.

In 1950 Hall, Cutlack & Harlock and Huntingdon Breweries merged to form East Anglian Breweries at Ely. In 1960 Steward and Patterson bought the brewery, but in 1967 they were taken over by Watney Mann and in 1969 Watney Mann closed Ely's last brewery, ending centuries of brewing in the city. The brewers left with a final flourish, brewing some Bona Cervisia – the best the old monks of Ely had to offer.

47. Ely's Two Maltings

Ely has two riverside maltings, one formerly owned by the Harlock family and one by the Hall family. Hall's Maltings is the older, dating from the 1760s and maintaining its original floors; it became a successful antiques business in 1986. The business, begun by Graham Peters and now run by his son, Tom, has sixty-five dealers sharing some 10,000 square feet, making it the largest in East Anglia and a major riverside attraction.

The Maltings public hall was built by Ebenezer William Harlock in 1868. In 1969, when Watney Mann closed the Ely brewery, Sir Harry Legge-Bourke, the Isle of Ely MP, negotiated the sale of the fire-damaged Maltings to Ely Urban District Council for £100, on condition

Waterside Antiques.

The Maltings.

that it was converted into a public hall. The recent loss of the Corn Exchange had made finding a public hall for Ely even more urgent, but despite that there was a strong local campaign in Ely not to convert the Maltings, instead to build a modern all-purpose public hall and sports hall on the edge of the Paradise. In the end the council voted 13 to 2 to go ahead and convert the Maltings into a new hall.

Ely architect Dennis Adams was responsible for the plans. In the main hall it is clearly seen from the walls and the position of the windows where the building once had three floors. The Maltings was officially opened by the Rt Hon. Peter Walker in October 1971. On 23 November 1973, as part of the thirteenth centenary celebrations for Ely, Queen Elizabeth II visited the city and was entertained to lunch at the Maltings, when it was announced that Ely would be given new letters patent and entitled officially to be called a city.

In 1974 the ownership of the Maltings passed to East Cambridgeshire District Council. The building has undergone many improvements over the years, including the building of a new riverside restaurant. In 2015 ownership of the building was transferred to the City of Ely Council, who now manage it.

48. Ely's Lost Pubs

Patrick Ashton's *Ely Inns*, published by the Ely Society in 2007, looks at the history of seventy-four public houses in Ely, although there may have well been some smaller ones through history that have gone unrecorded. Sixty-three of those listed are no longer pubs today, with thirty-two of the buildings demolished or changed beyond recognition, but thirty-one former pubs are still recognisable, with most being private residences.

That epitome of the market town inn, the Bell, can still be discerned on the High Street, above the modern Subway and Vodafone shop fronts, and the Black Bull at Waterside just about conceals its 300-year-history. The Chequers in Chequer Lane, now four small shops, served ale for over 300 years until its closure in 1958. The Club Inn, closed in 1975, still stands on the Market Place, as does the White Hart, which closed in 1986. The Dolphin on the corner of the High Street and Dolphin Lane, which closed in 1965, has a Victorian corner to the High Street but a much older side to Dolphin Lane, probably going back to the seventeenth century. The Dream Doors shop on the corner of Market Place and Fore Hill, for so many years Haylock's boot and shoe shop, was once the ancient Duke of York.

There were many pubs along Broad Street, including the Three Blackbirds, which was renovated into private residences in 1981 by the Ely Preservation Trust after 140 years as an alehouse. The Globe stood where the Basmati Indian restaurant now welcomes customers, while the Fortune Garden takeaway was the Coach and Horses until 1916. Spice City on Fore Hill was the Rose and Crown for 180 years until 1970.

From 1790 to 1913 the Queen's Head served people at Waterside, occupying one of the most prominent sites overlooking the river, while the Three Crowns at Crown Point, Waterside, was an important alehouse from 1790 to 1912 (it was also a residence and blacksmiths).

The King William IV was open for business from 1830 until 1962 on the corner of Lynn Road and Egremont Street, while the Peacock, with its arch through to a courtyard now containing Stable Mews, was on St Mary's Street from 1783 to 1955.

The former Bell Hotel, High Street.

The old White Lion, St Mary's Street.

The White Lion was one of the city's most important inns, associated in the mid-seventeenth century with Nicholas Mallabar, one time master of the workhouse or Spinning House, which employed many of the local poor in spinning wool. He was a wealthy man and owned several properties in the town. The White Lion closed in 1970 and is now a veterinary practice.

49. They Still Serve

The oldest inn in Ely is the Lamb Hotel. The original Lamb took its name from Agnus Dei, the Lamb of God, and was recorded in Bishop Fordham's survey of 1416. The Lamb had its own cockpit. In the late eighteenth century the Lamb stopped brewing its own beer and entered into an agreement with John Harlock to sell his ales. This allowed the inn to convert into a coaching inn, especially as Ely was now connected with turnpike roads.

In 1828–9 the Lamb was extensively rebuilt to take on the appearance it has today. When the railway came to Ely, the Lamb sent its own omnibus to and from the station to collect passengers. The Lamb is now a modern hotel catering for both visitors and locals.

A short distance from the Lamb, in St Mary's Street, is the Kings Arms, one of the oldest pubs in Ely, dating back to 1790, while the High Flyer on Newnham Street dates from the same time. Like most public houses today they serve food and provide entertainment for their customers.

West End public house, 2017.

The Minster, which has all the feel of an old established public house, was originally the Greyhound and owned between 1817 and 1914 by the Hills family. In 1944 it became the Minster Wine Vaults and in 1976 the Minster Tavern.

The Cutter dates from the new cut of the River Ouse in 1830, while the West End House has been in business on the corner of Chiefs Street and West End since 1839.

The Prince Albert was in Silver Street in 1842 but moved and was built on its present site in 1869, when housing was built for the militia, which probably gives the Fountain on the corner of Barton Square seniority in terms of age, as the building dates from 1848. It was closed in 1995 but saved by local businessman John Borland, who reopened it the next year and continues to run it as a free house.

The Royal Standard on Fore Hill demonstrates the changing pattern in the history of public houses. Opened in the 1870s, it doubled in size in 1969 when it took the adjoining premises, formerly occupied by Vernon Cross as Ye Olde Tea Rooms, which had its own museum. In recent years the Standard, like others, has built a reputation for its restaurant, as public houses adapt to stay in business.

The story of Ely's public houses is not entirely one of closures. In 1996 the Town House opened in Market Street; in May 2005 the Hereward opened almost opposite in Market Street in the converted former Cutlacks premises, and Ely's first micro pub, now the Drayman's Son, opened on Fore Hill in 2014 as the Liberty Belle.

The Drayman's Son, 2017.

50. Old Hereward Hall

Standing in a prominent corner of Barton Square at the bottom of the gallery, Old Hereward Hall was built between 1880 and 1881 by the Revd Richard Winkfield, headmaster of King's Ely. Along with Dean Merivale, Winkfield had reformed the governance of the school, which had been struggling financially, and in 1879 Queen Victoria approved the new arrangements for the school, which then became more commonly known as the King's School, rather than Ely Cathedral Grammar School. The new boarding house, which could accommodate sixty pupils and their masters, was built on the site of the old Green Man public house, formerly the Swann, and the one time seventeenth-century home of the Revd William Hitch, who features in the story of Oliver Cromwell's time in Ely.

Hereward Hall, as it was then, has a special place in Ely's wartime history. The King's School had seen its number of pupils decline because of the war and Chairman of Governors, Dean Lionel Blackburne, in 1941 seeing the need of the pupils of the Jews' Free School (JFS) who had been evacuated to Ely in 1939, offered the building to Enoch Bernstein, the head of the JFS, for a school. It was at one of the lowest moments in the history of the JFS, when the Brick Lane school had been destroyed in the Blitz, but from the summer of 1941 the boys and girls had the use of the building as a modern school. It transformed their stay in Ely.

Hereward Hall and the Porta.

In recent times more rooms have been skilfully added in the roof space, lit by dormer windows, and the building has been extended along Silver Street, creating a courtyard behind it.

51. Theological College

Few people may remember that the impressive Victorian building at Barton Square, now part of King's Ely, was once a theological college for the Anglican Church. The college was founded by Bishop James Woodford, Bishop of Ely from 1873–86, when he came to Ely. The building, which is adorned by a statue of the Bishop, dates from the same time as Hereward Hall, both being in red brick and complementing each other across Barton Square. The college had extensive gardens running along Barton Road up to the King's Ely playing field and they were often used for garden fêtes and community events. The grounds are now mainly occupied by Bishop Woodford House, the Diocese of Ely's Retreat and Conference Centre.

King's Ely has expanded onto the old Barton Farm behind the college with a complex that includes sports facilities and a new junior school. The school has over 1,000 students and under its current Principal, Mrs Sue Freestone, the first female head of the school, appointed in 2004, it is now one of the largest employers in the city and contributes hugely to the cultural, sporting and academic life of Ely and surrounding area.

Former Theological College.

DID YOU KNOW?

In around 1911 Canon Henry Leighton Goudge was Principal of the Theological College. With him was his eleven-year-old daughter, Elizabeth, who later won the Carnegie Medal in 1946 for her children's book, *The Little White Horse*. Elizabeth Goudge loved Ely, calling it 'The Home of Homes' and used life in the shadow of the cathedral as inspiration for her novel *The Dean's Watch*.

52. St Peter's Church

St Peter's is a lovely small church, plain on the outside but the glory inside is in the rood screen, one of the early works of Sir John Ninian Comper (1864–1960), famous for his highly decorative church furnishings.

Ely was growing after the arrival of the railway, particularly in the area close to the station. Historically the riverside area was a busy trading area, with basket-weaving yards, coal yards, brewing, public houses and some of the poorest housing in the city.

In 1889 Catharine Maria Sparke, widow of Canon Edward Bowyer Sparke, paid for a mission church to be established on Broad Street in memory of her husband.

Above: St Peter's Church rood screen.

Right: St Peter's 1914–18 war memorial.

Edward Bowyer Sparke was a very wealthy man who benefitted from the patronage of his father. Bishop of Ely from 1812–1836, Bishop Sparke was notorious for benefitting his family. It was said at the time that you could find your way around the fens and parts of Norfolk on a dark night by 'the number of little Sparkes along the road'. The second son of Bishop Bowyer Edward Sparke, Edward Bowyer Sparke was given the livings of both Littleport and Feltwell.

A mystery of St Peter's is why a name was erased from the First World War memorial plaque placed in the church by the solicitor Harold Archer in 1922. The memorial records the names of the boys he prepared for confirmation but later gave their lives in the Great War. One name recorded, however, was that of someone who subsequently returned to Ely several years later, and whose name was thus removed.

53. The Fountain

It is not always easy to think of a suitable way to commemorate great national occasions. Probably the most successful in Ely has been the creation of Jubilee Gardens in 2002 to mark the 60th year of Queen Elizabeth's reign, although when the scheme to create gardens on the site was first mooted it wasn't as a Jubilee project.

Faced with the Diamond Jubilee of Queen Victoria in 1897, the newly elected Ely Urban District Council, a body only in existence since 1895, chose to place a drinking fountain in the Market Place. The Market Place was the traditional assembly point in the city for national occasions and the obvious place for something that would be both decorative and practical.

The Victoria Jubilee Fountain, Market Place, c. 1908.

The Fountain, Archery Crescent, 2017.

Sadly it was never really popular with many people. The metal cups went missing and it was often dry. By the 1930s the Market Place was being used increasingly to park cars and it was thought by some that the fountain was getting in the way.

In 1939 it was decided to move the fountain and in the May of that year it was dismantled by Davis, the Ely stonemasons, and re-erected as a waterless feature on the green in front of the Archery Crescent bungalows.

Various attempts to have the fountain reinstalled on the Market Place have failed due to healthy and safety issues.

54. VR and ED

In 1891 Ely got a magnificent new post office on Market Street, on the corner of High Street Passage. There had been various kinds of post offices, one run by John Clements in the Market Place, and before the new post office was built it was at Minster Place. This was a building of red brick and of a size and eminence that added dignity to the town.

High above the door were the letters VR for Victoria Regina, so when Ernest Dingle built his impressive grocery emporium opposite in 1909, he had his initials, ED, placed high on his building facing those of VR.

Above: Victorian Post Office.

Left: Ernest Dingle's grocery emporium.

Nothing lasts forever and the post office closed in 1966, when a new post office was built on the other side of Market Street on the Market Place (this was demolished in 1997 to make way for the entrance to the new Cloisters shopping centre).

The Zasche family took the old post office premises and opened part of it as the City Cycle Centre, while Dingle's became Bennett's grocer, then Gay-Fem clothes shop, Brands Pet Store and, today, Costa Coffee.

55. Centre E

For a generation of young people an impressive building on Barton Road was Centre E, their youth club. Centre E was opened in 1968 by England International Rugby Union Player Dickie Jeeps, but it had an important place in Ely's history before that.

It was formerly known as the Drill Hall, built on the edge of the old militia drill and parade ground and opened by General R.M. Luckcock, Honorary Colonel of the Cambridgeshire Regiment of the Territorial Army, as their headquarters in May 1939.

In late 1941 the Cambridgeshire Regiment was sent overseas and arrived in Singapore in January 1942, only to be overwhelmed by the invading Japanese and forced to surrender. Members of the regiment were killed in the fighting and many others died in captivity on the infamous Death Railway.

Centre E.

The TA and the cadets continued to use the hall after the war and it was also a popular social venue for dances until the County Council acquired it as a new youth club. As youth activities were reduced over the years it went through various attempts to revitalise it with a new name, The Forum. For some years part of the building was used by the County Council as a Pupil Referral Unit, and the St John Ambulance Brigade also used it as their headquarters.

In 2015 the building was leased by a new charity, the Youth Ely Hub, at the instigation of Ely Councillor Elaine Griffin Singh, to be run as a youth and community venue, and at the time of writing it is proving a popular and busy venue again.

56. Royal Air Force Hospital

In the event of another war with Germany, which appeared increasingly likely during the 1930s, the Royal Air Force would have a major role and East Anglia would be in the front line. In 1937 approval was given for a hospital to serve the region and a site was chosen in north Ely. In 1939 building work began and the first wards were completed in June 1940.

In 1939, when war was declared, the Grange at Littleport, which was the Transport and General Workers' Union Convalescent Home, was requisitioned to provide care until the

Royal Air Force Hospital, *c.* 1990.

City crest at Princess of Wales Hospital, 2017.

Ely Hospital was ready. In August 1940 the hospital was declared open as the Royal Air Force General Hospital Ely, with 230 beds, and the Grange became an annex.

King George VI and Queen Elizabeth visited the hospital on 18 January 1941. By June 1943 further wards had increased the hospital's capacity to 527 beds.

From 1949 the hospital's bed numbers were reduced but civilian patients were admitted and treated. In 1968, in recognition of the high regard the community had for the hospital, the Urban District Council presented the City badge to the hospital, giving them the right to use it, and in 1977 the City Council bestowed the Freedom of the City on the hospital.

In July 1987, following a visit from Diana, the Princess of Wales, the hospital became officially The Princess of Wales Royal Air Force Hospital. Sadly, in 1992, the Ministry of Defence decided to close the hospital and sell the site for housing. Fortunately, the local campaign ACHE (Action Campaign Hospital Ely) saved a large part of the hospital, and part of the hospital grounds were redeveloped as Baird Lodge, a thirty-five-apartment care home named after Sir John Baird, former commanding officer of the RAF Hospital and later Surgeon General of the British Armed Forces from 1997–2000.

While some of the old wards and buildings of the RAF Hospital still remain, it is likely that redevelopment of the hospital will see them replaced by new buildings for the medical care of the community.

DID YOU KNOW?

Several famous figures were born in Ely because of the RAF connection: Rugby Union international and coach Sir Clive Woodward; rugby union international and county cricketer, a double blue at Cambridge University who also played for Ely City, Alastair Hignell; and actors Guy Pearce and Simon McCorkingdale.

57. Who Was J. Graven?

James Graven & Sons are still trading today, but under local businessman Jonathan James operates a number of petrol stations and forecourt shops.

The company began in 1860 with James Graven, an agricultural engineer based in what is now Castlehythe. After a bankruptcy in 1869, he recovered and specialised in steam tractors, even exporting steam engines to India.

The business moved to new works on Broad Street, where the name can be seen today in the recent housing development on the old factory site, named after James Graven's son, Charles Graven Court.

A meeting with Henry Ford in 1912 led to Graven's selling Ford tractors and cars and they were in business in Ely for many years until Jonathan James re-launched the family business in a new direction.

James Graven's former works in Broad Street.

58. Any Old Iron

In the second half of the nineteenth century Ely had an iron and brass foundry, the Eagle Works, on the bend of Downham Road, almost opposite West Fen Road. The foundry had been established in St Mary's Street in 1847 by W.F. Wilkinson, before moving to the new premises.

The Eagle foundry made agricultural implements, claiming the patent for the 'Self-Regulating Horse Hoe' as well as light and heavy waggons. Iron plates made by the company can still be seen in some old Ely streets. Ely builder Henry Youngs Morris, trading as H.Y. Morris & Son, later took the premises as their works and builders yard.

Wilkinson's cover plate. (© Pamela Blakeman)

59. The Corner Shop

While Charles Bass's shop in Chiefs Street near the West End has gone, the corner shop, now One Stop, so long associated with the Fletcher family, is a rare survivor, meeting the neighbourhood needs of a growing city.

One Stop, St John's Road, 2017.

Changing shopping habits along with the rise of the supermarkets has, since the late 1960s, seen the loss of many small shops and corner shops. Where once it was just a matter of popping out to a nearby shop for a pint of milk or a loaf of bread, it is not so convenient now. As a child, if I had a few pennies in my pocket I could stop at Harold Cowley's sweet shop on the corner of Egremont Street and Lynn Road, opposite the King William IV, and take on some supplies for the mile walk home up the Lynn Road. There was a small general store further along the Lynn Road, almost opposite the pathway through to New Barns Avenue, owned by the 8th Army veteran Percy Cross. One of the childhood delights of his small wooden shop were what we called 'apple ices' – slim frozen blocks of frozen fruit, which we loved on hot summer days.

There was another wooden grocery shop, little more than a shed, on Prickwillow Road, not far from the Majestic, owned by Mr Lowe. The Alps family had two shops not far away; one, next to the Majestic, was where Jim Alps sold radios, televisions and bicycles, while across the road, where the entrance to the Newnham Street car park is now, was Mrs Alps general stores, while just round the corner in New Barns Road was another shop next to the entrance to Paradise Ground. Further along New Barns Road, near the junction with Beech Lane, or Cemetery Lane as it was then, was Bowles shop. This is now Mrs Singh's Spar store, still serving the New Barns and High Barns area.

When High Barns was built in the late 1950s and early '60s, a small parade of shops was included, but they were not successful as the supermarket made them uncompetitive and there was not enough immediate local business to keep them going.

We referred to 'Gouldstone's corner' long after Mr Gouldstone had given up his shop on the corner of St Mary's Street and Downham Road. Further up St Mary's Street was

Porter's greengrocers, before getting to Jefferson's printers and then a corner shop at Cromwell Road, before reaching Lloyds general stores at West End.

For many years Mrs Moden kept a corner shop on Cambridge Road, at the junction with Barton Road, but that closed in the 1980s, while Silver Street had several small shops with one on the corner of Parade Lane and a small Co-op bakery next to Hereward Hall, handy as a tuck shop for hungry King's Ely students.

Fowlers shop stood at the bottom of Fore Hill, at the junction with Broad Street, while there was a small sub-post office along Station Road owned by Mrs Rogers. There were several shops along Broad Street, and in Waterside many people remember Monty Fielding's shop, now the boat chandlers.

60. Read All About It

Burrows newsagents has been a feature in Ely High Street longer than anyone can remember and is Ely's oldest family business. The business was founded by James F. Burrows, a newspaper reporter, in 1899. The first shop was small, on the end of the Butter Market overlooking the Market Place. From there he sold newspapers and magazines but also specialised in postcards, many of which he produced himself. The years before the First World War were a golden age for the postcard and they were sent in their millions.

Jeff Burrows at Burrows Newsagents, 2017.

1909. Yeas.

TO. SHEFFIELD VISITORS.

Ely's welcome to you is hearty and true,
And good luck with the rod and line,
Your health to renew ; other blessings not few,
And may you repeat it next time.

If you want a framed view, and a souvenir too,
Or if postcards are eagerly sought,
Go to BURROWS'S SHOP, do ; it's the
right thing for you,
And you'll be very pleased you have bought.

Anyone in Ely will tell you who BURROWS is, and where his Shop is.

It is situated on the south side of High Street, and his name BURROWS is on the Lamps outside the Shop.

He has beautiful views of the Cathedral, elegantly framed, a " Bob " apiece, smaller views are cheaper, also Souvenir match boxes with crest and view, albums, pin cushions, in fact it would take hours to mention all he sells in the Shop.

YOUR BEST PLAN IS TO PAY BURROWS A VISIT. His motto is

KEEP SMILING.

POST CARD

THE ADDRESS TO BE WRITTEN ON THIS SIDE.

Burrows' advertisement on the back of one of his postcards, 1909.

After about ten years James Burrows moved to a new larger shop on the southern side of the High Street, but in around 1914 he moved into premises close to the Lamb Hotel, which the family still own today.

James Burrows was a real livewire in the life of the city, always trying to promote the business of the town, and he served on the Urban District Council.

His son Percy took over the business, marrying Phyllis Sykes, who was also from an Ely business family. During the Second World War Percy served with the 11th Brigade Light Field Ambulance, being present at the liberation of Bergen-Belsen, an horrific experience which haunted him for years. While he was away James Burrows and his wife came out of retirement and, along with Phyllis, kept the shop running.

Percy's son Jeff took over the business and continues to run it, helped by his sister Ann and Ann's daughter Annabel, who also runs Burrows Bookshop in High Street Passage, which opened in 1994. Older readers will remember the late shop assistant 'Snakey' Blakewell selling the London evening papers and 'The Pink Un' football results paper to the crowds outside the Rex on a Saturday evening, which he did from 1938 until the cinema closed. Another long-serving member of staff, Tony Ransome, retired in 2017.

61. What's in a Name?

Ely has many old and interesting street names. The Gallery is named after a covered gallery that connected the Palace to the cathedral. This gallery is shown on Speed's Map of Ely dated 1610, and provided a covered private entrance and was above all the mud and filth of the street.

The Vineyards recalls the vineyards on that slope in medieval times and there were more vineyards in the Park. Butchers Row is derived from The Butchery and a reminder that in medieval times there were butchers' stalls there.

Angel Drove takes its name from the ancient Angel pub which stood on the corner of Station Road, once known as Bridge Road because of a stone bridge over the stream coming into the river from Cawdle Fen. The Angel was there in the seventeenth century but closed in 1995.

Potters Lane, one time The Potteries, is fairly obvious, making pots from local clay happened in many parts of this part of Ely, while there really was an ancient dovecot where Dovehouse Close stands, named Duffhousyard in early records. Castlehythe, delightfully spelled differently at either end, so Castelhythe, if you wish, recalls the stone castle built by Bishop Nigel that stood somewhere very close and may account for some of the old stone found in walls nearby. For a while this was Railway Terrace until renaming, and nearby Annesdale was Auntresdale in the fifteenth century.

The Gallery.

The Range and the old Militia Hospital.

Barton Road takes its name from the ancient Bishop's manor of Barton and generations of Ely people got their milk from Barton Farm and remember the Martin family who were last to farm the area until 1971, before King's Ely took over the land.

The Range and Parade Lane off Silver Street were directly linked to housing for members of the Militia, which had been revived in Ely in 1852 but left the city in 1908.

Brays Lane recalls an ancient family who owned the land there, while Nutholt Lane is a reference to the nutholt which lay to the north.

New Barns was an ancient manor owned by the Bishop and some of the land became the site of Ely's biggest interwar building project by the Urban District Council when New Barns Avenue was begun in 1929. So large was the scheme that the locals dubbed it 'China Town'. The area of Ely named the Butts, off Lynn Road, was where there were once archery butts.

Two former composers and organists at the cathedral are remembered in street names with the sixteenth-century Christopher Tye, who also became rector at Doddington, and John Amner (1579–1641), as are numerous Bishops including Kilkenny, Lonchamp, Northwold, Arundel, Thirlby, Wren, Laney, Gunning, Fleetwood, Mawson, Yorke, Allen, Compton, Chase and Wynn.

DID YOU KNOW?

St Martin's Walk is not named after a saint but the brand name of the jam and marmalade that was made between 1938 and 1959 in Granger's old jam factory, which opened in 1909 and once stood on that site.

St Martin's Walk.

62. Please Mr Postman

It is always a challenge for new names to be found for developments and streets. The developers want a name that sells properties, while the emergency services require names that will not be confused with somewhere else, and the City Council try and find a name with historic connexions or a theme, for example, local rivers or trees. Sometimes it is possible to bring back a lost name as, for example, with Winfarthing Court, off Ship Lane, which is partly on the old Winfarthing Lane, which had disappeared, and Little London, once a notorious area of poor housing along Lynn Road, which is now a modern housing development.

There are some recent examples of street names that have changed, with Cemetery Lane becoming the more genteel Beech Lane. It still runs alongside the cemetery, of course, but doesn't sound as if it does. Bull Lane, named after the long since closed public house, has reverted to Lisle Lane, which recalls the Lisle family who once owned that estate. Dolphin Lane, named after the old public house which once stood on the corner, was introduced to define one side of the Market Place.

But what of some of the ancient names that have gone? The most obvious is Steeple Row, which is now the High Street, while Steeple Row has been relegated to the path behind it, next to the cathedral.

High Street
Passage, 2017.

And what of Tallow Passage, which is now High Street Passage? In the early 1900s Market Street was Gaol Street, while Barton Road was Gaol Lane, although the top part of the road near Cambridge Road was Smock Mill Alley. And at the top of Cambridge Road, where did Buggs Hill go? West Fen Road was Cow Lane at this time.

Silver Street was for many years known as Walpole Lane, taking the name from the connexion with the Porta, which was known as the Walpole Gate, since it was built by William Walpole, the Prior of Ely sometime between 1396 and 1417, and before that it was Swallow or Swalugh Lane. Lardener's Lane, which was off Walpole Lane to the north, has been lost.

Sadly several of the old lanes off Broad Street have gone: Flax Lane, Baldocks Lane, Barkers Lane, Sedgwick, Ferours Lane and Monks Hythe, and when the gas works was built Croyles Lane became Gas Lane and now it is Back Lane.

In the early fifteenth century Chapel Lane was Cats Lane, Egremont Street was Acreman or Akyrman Street, and part of an ancient Roman road, Nutholt Lane, was Red Cross Lane, after the Red Cross that once stood near the Lynn Road junction, while Prickwillow Road was Common Road and Springhead Lane was Blithinghale Lane.

Do you know where Oyster Lane is? It is the private road alongside the Dean's Meadow that leads past the Canonry to the Deanery.

63. Tradition and Friendship

Ely is an ancient cathedral city and market town, but its colourful past has only included a Mayor since 1974, when it was officially granted city status by Her Majesty the Queen at the time of local government reorganisation, when the former Ely Urban District Council

Right: Councillor Richard Hobbs and
Mrs Pat Hobbs, Mayor and Mayoress, 2017.

Below: Town Crier competition, 2017.
Ely's Town Crier, Avril Hayter-Smith, is on
the left holding the bell.

joined with Ely Rural District Council and Newmarket Rural District Council to form East Cambridgeshire, and the old Urban District area became a parish. Councillor Richard Hobbs was elected Mayor in 2017 for the fourth time, which is a record for the city.

In 2001 the City Council decided to revive the role of the Town Crier, which had been in abeyance for many years. Avril Hayter-Smith, with her bellman Graham, has held the position since then and adds greatly to all civic occasions as well as hosting a popular Town Crier competition during the Ely Eel Festival.

Since 2006 the Maltings has housed a special tapestry designed by Ullrich Rosser and woven by Mona Lise Martinussen.

The special relationship, eventually becoming an official twinning, between Ely and the Danish City of Ribe began through the friendship of Colonel John Beckett, long-serving city and district councillor and Mayor from 1977–78, and the Revd Bitsch-Larsen of Ribe in 1956. Both ancient cities stand in the midst of flat arable and marsh land, with rivers, and graced by beautiful cathedrals, and have much in common. Ribe Court, one of Ely's first sheltered housing schemes, was named in honour of the friendship.

The twinning has endured through personal friendships maintained by regular exchange visits over the years as new faces have replaced the original pioneers.

Relationships with other European cities are also recognised and The Maltings has a Kempen Room, which was named after the East Cambridgeshire District Council's twinning with Kempen in Germany. This formal twinning began in 1978 and two years later the District Council also twinned with Orsay in France. In recognition they named a section of the Riverside Walk near the Maltings 'Quai d'Orsay'. Although the names remain in place, both twinnings officially ended in 2004, but the twinning based on friendship between Ely and Ribe endures.

Mona Lise Martinussen and Ribe Tapestry, 2016.

64. A City on a Hill

To commemorate the millennium, the City Council was faced with the age old dilemma of what kind of feature to create and where to put it. As with the celebration of Queen Victoria's Diamond Jubilee, the obvious place was the Market Place, but because of the high footfall, a structure was ruled out. The compromise was a sundial, designed and executed by Cambridgeshire sculptor Quin Hollick.

It is a human sundial which requires someone to stand in the centre and cast the shadow to tell the time. The dial is surrounded with many engraved stones depicting symbols associated with Ely – the city badge, the Ribe crest, East Cambridgeshire District Council badge, the three keys of the arms of the priory, the Cambridgeshire Regiment, the Showman's Guild, the Princess of Wales Royal Air Force Hospital, HMS *Walpole* (the warship adopted by the city during the Second World War), barrels and grapes (representing Ely's ancient vineyards), eels and an eel grigg, a windmill and a wheatsheaf.

The inscription in the centre of the sundial is particularly apt for the cathedral city of the Fens: 'Ye are the light of the world, A city set on a hill cannot be hid,' Matthew 5:14.

Of course, this particular city may hide many secrets; for example, are there tunnels under the city, as many people believe?

Do you know who wrote the following words: 'No man lives in Ely for a year without beginning to write a book, I do not say that all are published, but I swear that all are begun'? It was Hilaire Belloc in *Hills and the Sea*, quoted by Bernard Dorman in *The Story of Ely and its Cathedral*, published in 1945.

Centenary sundial on Market Place.

Acknowledgements

I have consulted so many sources over the years that it is not always possible to remember where everything came from. Certainly I acknowledge the research of Reg Holmes, Pamela Blakeman MBE and Mike Petty MBE. I thank Mike Young and all the members of the Ely Local History Publications Board for their knowledge and constructive criticism. I have always found the *Ely Standard* archive a huge source of information and similarly the extracts from the *Cambridge Chronicle*, collected by Muriel Wallace. Thanks to East Cambridgeshire District Council, the City of Ely Council, the Trustees of Ely Museum, and Tracey Harding and staff at Oliver Cromwell House. Thanks to the Dean and Chapter of Ely Cathedral, John Yates at St Peter's Church, Ann Powell and Mrs Sue Freestone, Principal of King's Ely, for access to the Old Palace gardens.

Unless stated otherwise all the photographs were taken by me, and the old photographs are from my collection; however, I would like to thank Pamela Blakeman for the photograph of the Wilkinson's iron plate, and The Stained Glass Museum, particularly the curator, Dr Jasmine Allen, for the photograph of part of the display. I thank David Heaps for access to take the photograph of Bentham's Monument and Richard Lee for Highflyer Farm. I have tried to mention sources of information in the text, but a general thanks to all those who have helped to answer queries and add snippets of information which can now be shared.